Theory Matters

Contents

1 Staves, clefs and notes — **4**

The notes of the treble clef — 4
Learning the notes of the treble clef — 4
Two common leger lines in the treble clef — 5
How to draw a treble clef — 6
Drawing other clefs — 6
The notes of the bass clef — 7
The notes of the alto and tenor (C) clefs — 7

2 Notes, rests, bars and barlines — **8**

Note values and relationships — 8
Writing notes and rests — 9
Dotted notes and rests — 10
Rhythm — 11
Bars and barlines — 11
Duple, triple and quadruple time — 11
Beating time — 12

3 Simple time signatures — **13**

What the numbers mean — 13
How to choose a simple time signature — 14
Placing your time signature on the st — 15

4 Putting notes into bars — **6**

Getting the maths right — 6
Grouping quavers and semiquavers into beats — 16
Anacrusis (up-beat) — 17
Triplets — 18

5   *A compound time signature:* $\frac{6}{8}$ **19**

When to use $\frac{6}{8}$ time   19
Grouping notes in $\frac{6}{8}$ time   20

6   *Sharps, flats and naturals*   **21**

Tones and semitones   21
Sharps, flats and naturals   21
Accidentals   22
Writing accidentals on the stave   22

7   *Scales, keys and key signatures*   **23**

Major scales   23
Major keys and key signatures   24
The order of sharps and flats in key signatures   25
Writing key signatures on the stave   26
Key signatures in the alto and tenor (C) clefs   26
Minor scales   27
Minor keys and key signatures   28
Accidentals in minor keys   29
Relative majors and minors   29
What is the key of this piece?   30
The pentatonic scale   31
Modes   31
The names of the notes of the scale   32

8   *Intervals*   **33**

9   *All about chords*   **34**

What is a chord?   34
Chord inversions (rearranging chords)   34
Patterns with chords   35
Naming chords   35
Primary chords   36
Secondary chords   36
Working out chords   37
Using chord symbols   37
Chords in common keys   38
Using chords in the Aeolian and Dorian modes   38
Cadences   39

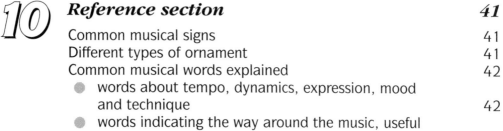

10 *Reference section* **41**

Common musical signs 41
Different types of ornament 41
Common musical words explained 42
 • words about tempo, dynamics, expression, mood
   and technique 42
 • words indicating the way around the music, useful
   supporting words and phrases 43
 • words for instruments, singers and their groups 43
 • words for musical styles and genres 44
 • words about form and structure 46
Words and rhythms 47
Keyboard chart 48

Heinemann Educational Publishers
Halley Court, Jordan Hill, Oxford OX2 8EJ
a division of Reed Educational & Professional Publishing Ltd

OXFORD   MELBOURNE   AUCKLAND
JOHANNESBURG   BLANTYRE   GABORONE
IBADAN   PORTSMOUTH (NH) USA   CHICAGO

Heinemann is a registered trademark of Reed Educational & Professional Publishing Ltd

© Marian Metcalfe, 1997

First published 1997

01 00 99 98   10 9 8 7 6 5 4 3 2

British Library Cataloguing in Publication Data
A catalogue record for this book is available from the British Library

ISBN 0 435 81025 1

Typeset and designed by Artistix, Thame, Oxon
Music typesetting by Halstan & Co, Amersham, Bucks
Printed and bound in Great Britain by The Bath Press, Bath
Cover designed by The Point

1 Staves, clefs and notes

Music is written on sets of five lines called **staves**. A **clef** (key) is placed at the beginning of each stave. There are several different clefs, and the positions of the notes on the stave change for each one.

Do not try to learn the notes of all the staves at once. Learn the notes for the **treble clef** and the **bass clef** and look the others up when you need them.

The treble clef is used for the notes in the upper half of the keyboard. The bass clef is used for the notes in the lower half of the keyboard.

The C in the middle of the keyboard is called **middle C**. Middle C appears in both clefs.

The notes of the treble clef

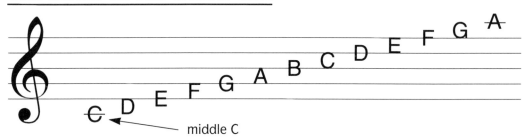

middle C

Things to notice:
- the notes use the lines and spaces alternately
- all the notes walk up the stave in alphabetical order *but*
- they only use the first seven letters of the alphabet *so*
- when they get to G they start again at A.

If you run out of lines, you draw an extra little line and put the note you want on it.

These extra lines are called **leger lines**. (More information about leger lines is found on page 5.)

Learning the notes of the treble clef

Use your left hand to help you remember the notes. Hold your hand out flat in front of you with the fingers spread wide. Keeping your hand flat, turn it 90° so your thumb points to the floor. Bend your wrist to bring the back of your hand round to face you so that you can see it.

This is your portable note learner.

Each of your five fingers is like a line of the stave, and the spaces between your fingers are the spaces between the lines. Imagine you have a note round each finger like a ring, and you are holding one between each finger (see diagram on page 5).

Your left hand portable note learner

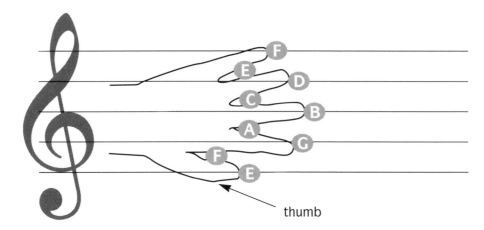

thumb

Starting with your thumb:

The line (finger) notes are **E G B D F.**

> Learn *Every* *Good* *Boy* *Deserves* *Fun* to remind you.

The space (space between the fingers) notes are **F A C E.**

> Learn that the space notes spell the words *FACE*.

Two common leger lines in the treble clef

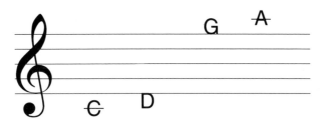

The two notes underneath the stave are **C** and **D**. They say *Can Do*.

> **C** has a leger line through the middle of it. Remember this is **middle C**.

> **D** hangs below the stave with nothing to support it. So it should touch the bottom line.

The two notes above the stave are **G** and **A**. They say *Get Active*.

> **G** sits on the top of the stave touching the top line.

> **A** has a leger line through the middle of it.

How to draw a treble clef

Step 1
This clef is also called the **G** clef. It curls round G's line. Start drawing the G clef with a little blob just below G's line.

Step 2
Take your blob up to the middle line and curve it round a little.

Step 3
Now bring it down to the bottom line and curve it round again.

Step 4
Curl your line right up through the stave and a little bit above, and hook it over.

Step 5
Cut your clef down through the middle like a jam roll, and let a little bit of jam hang on the bottom of your cut in a blob.

Drawing other clefs

Drawing the bass clef
This clef is also called the **F** clef. It curls round F's line. Start drawing the bass clef on the second to top line with a blob. Curve the line towards the left and up to the top line. Now bring it round and down. Add two dots in the top two spaces.

Drawing the alto (C) clef
The printed alto clef is shown below. If you prefer to write something simpler, a capital K with an extra line IK is also correct. Put the middle of the K on the middle line.

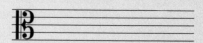

(for the **tenor** clef see page 7)

Now practise drawing clefs yourself.

The notes of the bass clef

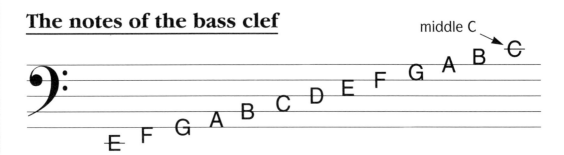

middle C

The line notes are **G B D F A**.

> Learn *Greed Brings Disaster For All* to remind you.

The space notes are **A C E G**.

> Learn *All Cows Eat Grass* to remind you.

The two notes underneath the stave are **E** and **F**. They say *Eat Fruit*.

> **E** has a leger line through it.

> **F** hangs below the stave with nothing to support it. So it should touch the bottom line.

The two notes above the stave are **B** and **C**. They say *Be Careful*.

> **B** sits on the top of the stave touching the top line.

> **C** has a leger line through it. Remember this is **middle C**.

The notes of the alto and tenor (C) clefs

You are unlikely to use these clefs unless you play the viola, the cello or the trombone, but it is a good idea to understand how they work.

The alto and tenor clefs look exactly the same, but they are placed on different lines of the stave. Whichever line the clef is placed on becomes **middle C** and the notes are worked out from there.

Alto clef notes (for viola)   Tenor clef notes (for cello and trombone)

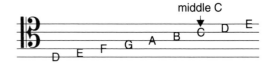

Notes, rests, bars and barlines

Notes have different shapes to show whether they are long or short. Each note also has a matching **rest** to show **silence**. Each note lasts for a different number of beats.

Note values and relationships

Note name	Note shape	Rest	Usually lasts for
Semibreve	o	* ▬	4 beats
Minim	𝅝	▬	2 beats
Crotchet	♩	𝄽 or 𝄽	1 beat
Quaver	♪	𝄾	$\frac{1}{2}$ beat
Semiquaver	♬	𝄿	$\frac{1}{4}$ beat

*When a *whole* bar needs a rest in $\frac{2}{4}$ $\frac{3}{4}$ $\frac{4}{4}$ or $\frac{6}{8}$ time (see sections 3 and 5 on time signatures), a *semibreve rest* is used.

Another way of understanding note values is to look at how they relate to each other.

Semibreve	o			
Minims	𝅗𝅥		𝅗𝅥	
Crotchets	♩	♩	♩	♩
Quavers	♫	♫	♫	♫
Semiquavers	♬♬	♬♬	♬♬	♬♬

Writing notes and rests

Notes and rests should be drawn carefully so that their meaning is clear.
Do not make notes and rests too large or too small. Fit them neatly on to the stave.

It matters whether stems go on the right of the note or on the left of the note. It also matters whether stems point up or hang down.

Learn the correct way to write stems.

Writing notes

Line notes should circle round their line without touching the line above or the line below.

Space notes should fill the entire space, but not go over the line above or the line below.

Things to remember:
- stems on notes go up on the right
- stems on notes go down on the left
- stems on notes go up when the note is below the middle line
- stems on notes go down when the note is above the middle line
- stems on notes go either way when the note is on the middle line.

Line notes   **Space notes**

Beams (joining lines) for quavers and semiquavers should be written at a slight angle so that they are not muddled with the lines of the stave.

* These stems could also go up as the notes lie evenly on each side of the middle line. Both stems must go the same way.

Writing rests

Rests need special attention. Draw them carefully so their meaning is clear.

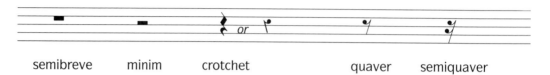

semibreve   minim   crotchet   quaver   semiquaver

- semibreve and minim rests are placed in the third space up
- semibreve rests *hang from the line*. Minim rests *sit on the line*
- heads of quaver rests and alternative crotchet rests are also placed in the third space up
- the top head of semiquaver rests is placed in the third space up.

Dotted notes and rests

A dot written after a note makes the note half as long again.

For example: a note normally worth 2 beats equals 3 beats if dotted
a note normally worth 1 beat equals $1\frac{1}{2}$ beats if dotted.

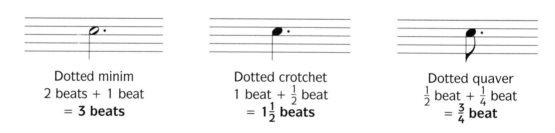

Dotted minim	Dotted crotchet	Dotted quaver
2 beats + 1 beat	1 beat + $\frac{1}{2}$ beat	$\frac{1}{2}$ beat + $\frac{1}{4}$ beat
= **3 beats**	= **$1\frac{1}{2}$ beats**	= **$\frac{3}{4}$ beat**

Rests can be dotted too. They are also worth $1\frac{1}{2}$ times their original length.

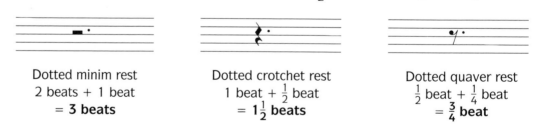

Dotted minim rest	Dotted crotchet rest	Dotted quaver rest
2 beats + 1 beat	1 beat + $\frac{1}{2}$ beat	$\frac{1}{2}$ beat + $\frac{1}{4}$ beat
= **3 beats**	= **$1\frac{1}{2}$ beats**	= **$\frac{3}{4}$ beat**

Rhythm

All music has rhythm. Usually the rhythm is based on a steady **pulse**. Some beats are regularly stronger than others. These regular strong beats help to move the music onwards.

Bars and barlines

A **barline** is placed *before* each strong beat. The barlines divide the stave up into **bars**. Each bar will usually have the same number of beats in it. When you add up the number of beats in each bar you will know if the music is in two time, three time or four time. A **double barline** is used at *the end* of a piece of music.

Duple, triple and quadruple time

If the strong beat falls on every 2nd beat we say that there are **2** beats in a bar and the music is in **two time**. In music this is called **duple time**.

This number tells us there are 2 beats in each bar. For more information about these numbers see Section 3, page 13.

barline   barline   double barline
at the end

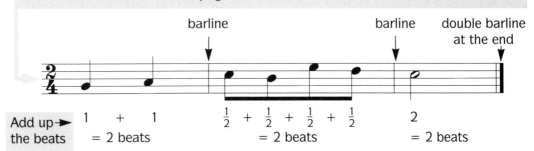

Add up → 1   +   1 $\frac{1}{2}$ + $\frac{1}{2}$ + $\frac{1}{2}$ + $\frac{1}{2}$ 2
the beats   = 2 beats   = 2 beats   = 2 beats

Duple time: 2 beats in every bar

If the strong beat falls on every 3rd beat we say that there are **3** beats in a bar and the music is in **three time**. In music this is called **triple time**.

This number tells us there are 3 beats in each bar. For more information about these numbers see Section 3, page 13.

barline   barline   double barline
at the end

Add up → 1 + 1 + 1   1   + $\frac{1}{2}$ + $\frac{1}{2}$ + $\frac{1}{2}$ + $\frac{1}{2}$ 3
the beats   = 3 beats   = 3 beats   = 3 beats

Triple time: 3 beats in every bar

11

If the strong beat falls on every 4th beat we say that there are **4** beats in a bar and the music is in **four time**. In music this is called **quadruple time**.

This number tells us there are 4 beats in each bar. For more information about these numbers see Section 3, page 13.

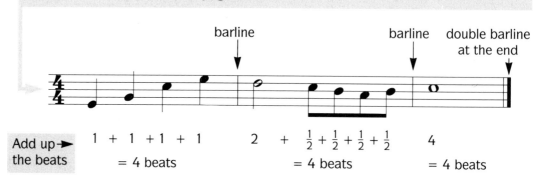

Add up →
the beats

$1 + 1 + 1 + 1$ $2 +$ $\frac{1}{2} + \frac{1}{2} + \frac{1}{2} + \frac{1}{2}$ 4

= 4 beats   = 4 beats   = 4 beats

Quadruple time: 4 beats in every bar

Beating time

When you need a signal to keep your group together, or to show them a speed (**tempo**) without making a noise such as clapping or counting aloud, you can beat time.

These are the directions for beating time. Follow the shapes in the air using your right hand.

2 beats in a bar   3 beats in a bar   4 beats in a bar

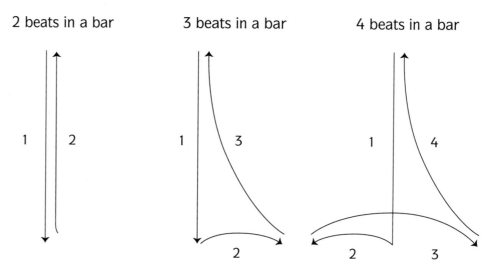

3 Simple time signatures

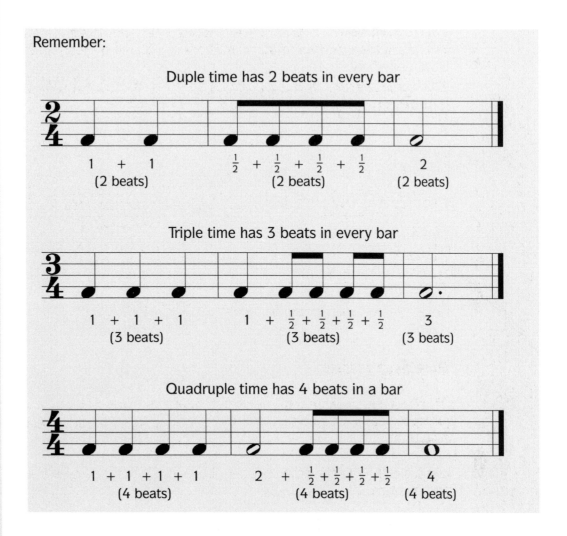

Remember:

Duple time has 2 beats in every bar

1 + 1 (2 beats) $\frac{1}{2} + \frac{1}{2} + \frac{1}{2} + \frac{1}{2}$ (2 beats) 2 (2 beats)

Triple time has 3 beats in every bar

1 + 1 + 1 (3 beats) 1 + $\frac{1}{2} + \frac{1}{2} + \frac{1}{2} + \frac{1}{2}$ (3 beats) 3 (3 beats)

Quadruple time has 4 beats in a bar

1 + 1 + 1 + 1 (4 beats) 2 + $\frac{1}{2} + \frac{1}{2} + \frac{1}{2} + \frac{1}{2}$ (4 beats) 4 (4 beats)

What the numbers mean

Notice that at the start of a piece of music (just before the notes begin) there are two numbers one above the other. This is called the **time signature**.

In **simple time** the top number tells you how many beats there are in the bar.

In **simple time** the bottom number tells you what sort of beat to count.

(NB There is another type of time called **compound time** where this does not happen, but you do not need to think about this yet. It is explained in Section 5.)

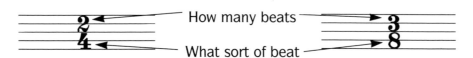

How many beats

What sort of beat

The top number

How many beats in the bar?

2 means 2 beats in a bar

3 means 3 beats in a bar

4 means 4 beats in a bar

The bottom number

What length are the beats?

4 means crotchet beats (the most common)

2 crotchets | 3 crotchets | 4 crotchets

8 means quaver beats

2 quavers | 3 quavers | 4 quavers

2 means minim beats

2 minims | 3 minims | 4 minims

Common time signatures

These are the ones you need to know:

2 3 4 2 3 3
4 4 4 2 2 8

Can you remember what they mean?

How to choose a simple time signature

1 Look back at pages 11 and 12 and read the section on rhythm again. Remember that every piece has some beats stronger than others.

2 Now decide which beats are the strong beats in the piece.
   - If you are listening to a piece try tapping silently on your knee in time with the strong beats.
   - If you are composing a piece, try singing it to yourself and tapping your knee in time. You may need to do this several times before you have a steady beat.

3　Next say '**one**' to yourself as you tap the strong beat. Keep counting and see how far you get before it's time to say 'one' again on the next strong beat. Say:

> '**one** two, **one** two, **one** two, **one** two' *or*
>
> '**one** two three, **one** two three, **one** two three, **one** two three' *or*
>
> '**one** two three four, **one** two three four, **one** two three four, **one** two three four.'

One of these patterns is likely to fit your piece. The top figure of your time signature will be 2, 3 or 4.

Choose 4 for your bottom figure unless you have a special reason to choose something else.

Now you have a time signature of:　$\frac{2}{4}$　$\frac{3}{4}$　or　$\frac{4}{4}$

Placing your time signature on the stave

There are three signs or groups of signs which are placed at the beginning of the first stave in a piece of music.

1　The **clef** (see page 6)
  - The clef is always placed first.
  - Every stave must have a clef placed first.

2　The **key signature** (see page 24)
  - The key signature is always placed second, immediately after the clef.
  - Every stave must have its key signature placed second.
    (NB *Not every piece has a key signature.*)

3　The **time signature** (see page 13)
  - The time signature is always placed third, immediately after the key signature.
  - The time signature is written *only once* on the first stave.
  - Do not write the time signature again unless the time changes.

Putting notes into bars

Getting the maths right

Remember: a time signature tells you how many beats there are in each bar. It also tells you what length the beats are (see page 14).

Each bar must add up to the correct number of beats. So:

$\frac{2}{4}$ must add up to 2 crotchets

beat 1 2 1 2 1 2 1 2

$\frac{3}{4}$ must add up to 3 crotchets

beat 1 2 3 1 2 3 1 2 3 1 2 3

$\frac{4}{4}$ must add up to 4 crotchets

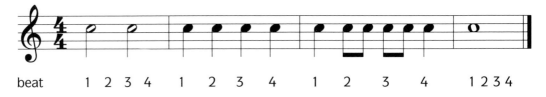

beat 1 2 3 4 1 2 3 4 1 2 3 4 1 2 3 4

Always check that each bar adds up correctly.

Grouping quavers and semiquavers into beats

Learn the grouping rule:

> Notes with tails should be joined together with beams to make separate beats.

Crotchet beat examples:

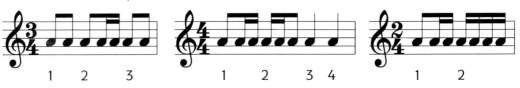

1 2 3   1 2 3 4   1 2

You have just learnt the grouping rule that notes with tails should be joined together to make separate beats BUT sometimes a whole *bar* of quaver notes all join together.

examples:

In $\frac{4}{4}$ time half a bar of quaver notes often join together i.e. beats 1 and 2, or beats 3 and 4 but *not* beats 2 and 3.

examples:

Examples of grouping

Anacrusis (up-beat)

Sometimes a bar does not begin on the first beat, but begins with an up-beat or **anacrusis** leading to the next bar. When this happens, its value is taken out of the last bar of the piece. For example:

Anacrusis is worth 1 crotchet, so the last bar is minus 1 crotchet.

Anacrusis is worth 1 quaver, so the last bar is minus 1 quaver.

Triplets

In simple time the beats normally divide into two or four. For example, a crotchet usually divides into two quavers or perhaps four semiquavers. However, sometimes in simple time a beat needs to be divided into three. When this happens the three notes are called a **triplet**.

A figure 3 is placed over or under the triplet to show that there are meant to be three notes in that beat. A curved line called a **slur** is often used too.

Any size beat can have a triplet.

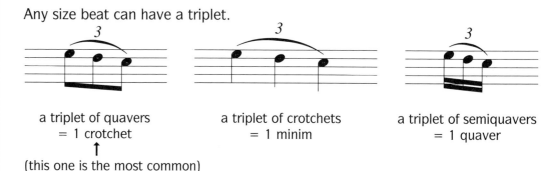

| a triplet of quavers
= 1 crotchet | a triplet of crotchets
= 1 minim | a triplet of semiquavers
= 1 quaver |

↑
(this one is the most common)

Playing a triplet

To play a triplet simply fit the three notes into the time of the beat. The music below is part of a piano piece which contains a triplet. *Can you spot it?*

Minuet by Mozart

5 A compound time signature: $\frac{6}{8}$

Compound time has dotted note beats instead of ordinary beats. Look at the examples below:

(triplet)

Example A has a time signature of 2 crotchets and is in **simple duple time**.

Example B has a time signature of 2 dotted crotchets and is in **compound duple time**. However, there is no time signature to represent dotted beats, so the 2 dotted crotchets are broken down into 6 quavers, and the time signature of $\frac{6}{8}$ is used.

Remember in $\frac{6}{8}$ time:

- there are 6 quavers in every bar
- there are only *2 beats* in every bar
- the 2 beats are *dotted* beats
- there are 3 quavers to each beat
- triplet signs are not needed in this time.

When to use $\frac{6}{8}$ time

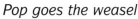

$\frac{6}{8}$ time is often used for jigs and other pieces needing a skipping rhythm.
The beginning of two famous pieces using $\frac{6}{8}$ time are printed below.

Pop goes the weasel

Half a pound of tup-pen-ny rice, half a pound of trea - cle . . .

The Skye Boat Song

Speed bon-ny boat like a bird on the wing, O - ver the sea to Skye.

Sing these two songs to yourself and listen to the skipping rhythms in your head.

Grouping notes in $\frac{6}{8}$ time

In $\frac{6}{8}$ time quavers and semiquavers join together in their beats as they do in simple time. There are no exceptions to this rule.

Look back at the two songs in $\frac{6}{8}$ on the previous page. The dotted crotchet beats are clearly seen in the way the quavers and semiquavers group together. Now compare the two examples below.

Example A is in $\frac{3}{4}$ time, that is 3 crotchet beats per bar.

Example B is in $\frac{6}{8}$ time, that is 2 dotted crotchet beats per bar.

The beats in each bar both add up to the same number of quavers, but the different groupings match the time signature each example is using, and show whether they have 3 simple beats or 2 compound (dotted) beats per bar.

It is important to keep the half-way mark in the bar clear in $\frac{6}{8}$ time. This will always happen if you join the notes together in their beats.

Rests (see page 10) follow the same rules as notes. For example:

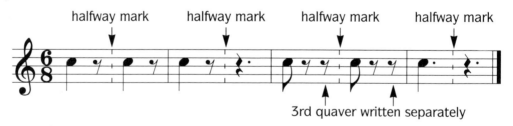

- The halfway mark is always kept clear to show the two beats clearly.
- Because each beat in $\frac{6}{8}$ time is a dotted crotchet (crotchet plus quaver) the rest for the *quaver* is always written separately (see bar 3). The dot can be used with the crotchet rest when the whole beat is a rest (see last bar).

As in simple times a whole bar's rest is always a semibreve rest even in $\frac{6}{8}$ time (see page 8).

Other compound times are outside the scope of this book.

Sharps, flats and naturals

Tones and semitones

The smallest distance in pitch between any two notes on the keyboard is called a **semitone**.

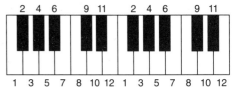

The keyboard

Look at the diagram of the keyboard opposite.
You will see that the notes have been numbered.

Next-door notes are a semitone apart. In the diagram there are semitones between notes 1-2, notes 2-3, 3-4, 4-5, 5-6, 6-7, 7-8, and so on. Note that there are two 'white' semitones on the keyboard: between 7 and 8, and between 12 and 1. All the other semitones lie between a white note and the next nearest black note.

Two next-door semitones make a **tone**. In the diagram there are tones between notes 1-3, notes 2-4, 3-5, 4-6, 7-9, and so on.

Sharps, flats and naturals

The sign ♯ is a sharp. Sha**R**ps **R**aise notes one semitone to the next note on the **R**ight.

Find each example written below on the pictures of the keyboard above and on page 22.

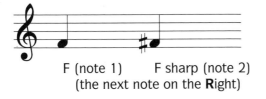

F (note 1)   F sharp (note 2)
(the next note on the **R**ight)

C (note 8)   C sharp (note 9)
(the next note on the **R**ight)

(On the guitar you will finger the next fret up, and on the violin and cello you will need to finger a little closer to the bridge.)

The sign ♭ is a flat. **FL**ats **L**ower notes one semitone to the next note on the **L**eft.

Find each example written below on the pictures of the keyboard above and on page 22.

B (note 7)   B flat (note 6)
(the next note on the **L**eft)

E (note 12)   E flat (note 11)
(the next note on the **L**eft)

(On the guitar you will finger the next fret down. On the violin and the cello you will need to move a little further from the bridge. You may even need to finger the next string down.)

A natural sign (♮) is used to cancel a sharp or a flat.

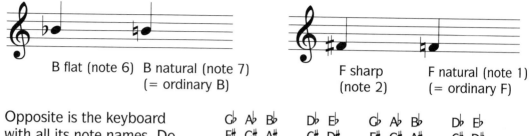

B flat (note 6)   B natural (note 7)
(= ordinary B)

F sharp
(note 2)

F natural (note 1)
(= ordinary F)

Opposite is the keyboard with all its note names. Do not worry about the black notes having two names at this stage (see Section 7 for the reason).

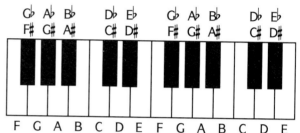

Accidentals

The family name for sharps, flats and naturals is **accidentals**.

Writing accidentals on the stave

Accidentals need to be written very carefully. They must sit before their note on the same line or space.

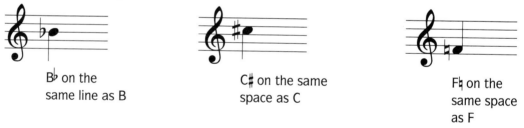

B♭ on the
same line as B

C♯ on the same
space as C

F♮ on the
same space
as F

An accidental lasts for the rest of the bar. It *needs to be written again* after the barline.

F♯ F♯F♯ G A   A G F♯G G   F♯ E F♯G E   D D E F♯

Look at the example above. Not every note labelled F♯ underneath has a sharp sign in front of its note on the music. This is because only the first F♯ in each bar needs an accidental.

Remember: an accidental lasts for the rest of the bar.

7 Scales, keys and key signatures

Most music is composed using a particular pattern of notes called a **scale**. There are many different types of scale, each with its own special pattern. The scale patterns are usually made up of tones and semitones (look back at page 21 for semitones and tones). Once you know the pattern, you can work out a scale starting on any note.

Two very popular patterns are the **major scale** pattern and the **minor scale** pattern. Every note has its major and its minor scale.

Major scales

Major scales have the following pattern of tones and semitones:

tone tone semitone tone tone tone semitone

They also always have their letter-names in order, with none missing. On the keyboard below, you will see the pattern of tones (T) and semitones (S) in the major scale of C.

C major scale

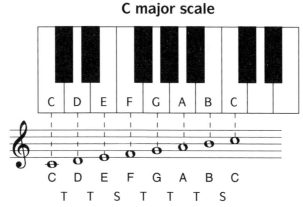

In order to keep the pattern of tones and semitones correct, accidentals (see page 22) are used.

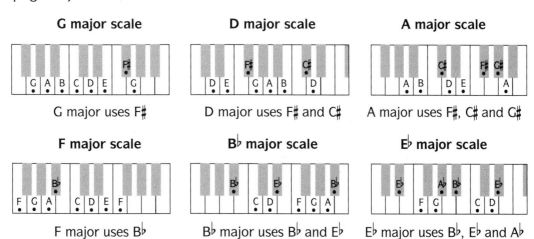

G major scale	D major scale	A major scale
G major uses F♯	D major uses F♯ and C♯	A major uses F♯, C♯ and G♯

F major scale	B♭ major scale	E♭ major scale
F major uses B♭	B♭ major uses B♭ and E♭	E♭ major uses B♭, E♭ and A♭

Major keys and key signatures

All major scales must use the major scale pattern of tones and semitones. This means that, except for C major, they all need at least one sharp or flat. To save writing the sharps or flats every time they are needed, they are grouped together and written immediately after the clef at the beginning of every line of the stave (see page 15).

This group of sharps or flats is called the **key signature** and indicates the **key** (or scale) of the piece.

The key signature tells a musician which scale or key the piece uses, and which note is the key note. The key note is always the first note of the scale. The major keys and their key signatures in the treble and bass clefs are shown below.

C major
C major has no sharps or flats

C D E F G A B C

G major
G major has one sharp – F♯

G A B C D E F♯ G

D major
D major has 2 sharps – F♯ and C♯

D E F♯ G A B C♯ D

A major
A major has 3 sharps – F♯, C♯ and G♯

A B C♯ D E F♯ G♯ A

E major
E major has 4 sharps – F♯, C♯, G♯, D♯

E F♯ G♯ A B C♯ D♯ E

F major
F major has one flat – B♭

F G A B♭ C D E F

B♭ major
B♭ major has two flats – B♭ and E♭

B♭ C D E♭ F G A B♭

E♭ major
E♭ major has 3 flats – B♭, E♭ and A♭

E♭ F G A♭ B♭ C D E♭

A♭ major
A♭ major has 4 flats – B♭, E♭, A♭, D♭

A♭ B♭ C D♭ E♭ F G A♭

24

The order of sharps and flats in key signatures

Look carefully at the key signatures of the major scales on page 24. Notice that the order of the sharps or the order of the flats in each one is always the same.

F is always the first sharp, C is always the second sharp, and so on. In the same way, B is always the first flat, E is always the second flat, and so on.

The full reason for this is outside the scope of this book, but if you are interested in patterns and relationships, you may like to notice that the next sharp scale is always found on the 5th note of the one before (e.g. D with 2 sharps begins on the 5th note of G with 1 sharp), and the next flat scale is always found on the 4th note of the one before (e.g. B♭ with 2 flats begins on the 4th note of F with 1 flat).

Because the order of the flats or sharps in a key signature is always the same, it is easy to memorize the order they are written in.

Order of sharps: **F   C   G   D   A   E   B**

You may like to learn this sentence to remind you:

Following Christmas, Grandpa Dieted And Exercised Bravely

Order of flats: **B   E   A   D   G   C   F**

Learn the following sentence to remind you:

Being Elderly, Aunty Daisy Got Chocolate Free

It is also worth noticing that the order of the sharps is the same as the order of the flats backwards.

Sharps ➡	F	C	G	D	A	E	B	
	B	E	A	D	G	C	F	⬅ Flats

It does not matter how you remember the order of the sharps and flats in a key signature, but it is very useful to know it by heart.

Writing key signatures on the stave

As well as always being in the same order, the sharps and flats of key signatures are always written in the same place on the stave. For example: F sharp is *always* written in these positions in the treble and bass clefs:

(top line)   (4th line)

and B flat is *always* written in these positions:

(3rd line)   (2nd line)

Once a key signature is in place, it changes every appearance of the notes involved *no matter what pitch they are written at*.

For example, the key signature of one sharp (F) changes all these Fs to F♯s:

F sharp   F sharp   F sharp   F sharp

And the key signature of one flat (B) changes all these Bs to B♭s:

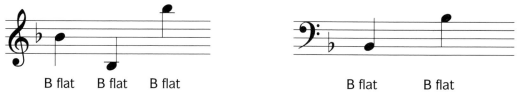

B flat B flat B flat   B flat B flat

So you can see that writing a key signature at the beginning of every stave saves writing a lot of accidentals (see page 22).

Key signatures in the alto and tenor (C) clefs

If you play an instrument which uses these clefs, knowing where the sharps or flats lie on the stave may be useful:

Alto clef   F♯ C♯ G♯ D♯   Tenor clef   F♯ C♯ G♯ D♯

B♭ E♭ A♭ D♭   B♭ E♭ A♭ D♭

Minor scales

There are two types of minor scale. They are called:

harmonic: usually used for backing chords, harmony etc.

melodic: usually used for melodies.

They have slightly different patterns of tones and semitones.

Here is the harmonic minor scale pattern:

tone semitone tone tone semitone (tone + semitone) semitone

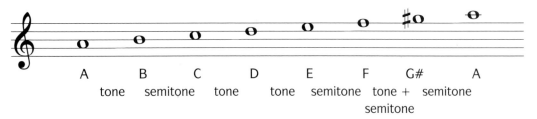

A	B	C	D	E	F	G#	A
tone	semitone	tone		tone	semitone	tone +	semitone
						semitone	

The melodic minor scale pattern of tones and semitones is *different ascending and descending*. Here it is *ascending* (going up):

tone semitone tone tone tone tone semitone

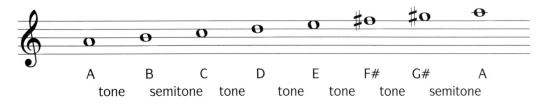

| A | B | C | D | E | F# | G# | A |
| tone | semitone | tone | | tone | tone | tone | semitone |

And here it is *descending* (coming down):

tone tone semitone tone tone semitone tone

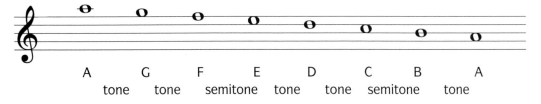

| A | G | F | E | D | C | B | A |
| tone | tone | semitone | tone | | tone | semitone | tone |

In both minor scales the 3rd note is one semitone lower than the 3rd note in the major scale which starts on the same note.

This '**minor 3rd**' is the most important feature in hearing whether a piece of music is major or minor.

Minor keys and key signatures

Like major scales, all minor scales except for A minor need at least one sharp or flat to keep the pattern of tones and semitones correct. (NB Harmonic and melodic minor scales have the *same* key signatures.)

As with major scales, to save writing the sharps or flats every time they are needed, they are grouped together and written as a key signature immediately after the clef at the beginning of every line of the stave (see page 15).

The key signature tells a musician which scale or key the piece uses, and which note is the key note. The key note is always the first note of the scale.

The minor keys and their key signatures in the treble and bass clefs are shown below. (NB All scales are *harmonic* minors.)

*See page 29 for an explanation of why each minor scale has an extra accidental which is not written in the key signature.

Accidentals in minor keys

To keep the pattern of tones and semitones correct in minor scales, accidentals are added to some notes.

These extra accidentals have nothing to do with the key signature. They are needed in addition to the key signature to keep the correct pattern.

In the **harmonic minor scale**, the accidental raises the 7th note one semitone.

In the **melodic minor scale**, the accidentals raise the 6th *and* the 7th notes ascending, and lower them again (back to their key signature notes) descending.

Do not worry about accidentals in minor keys. When you are looking at music, extra accidentals can help you decide whether a piece is in a major or a minor key.

When you are composing a piece in a minor key, use your ear to decide whether your piece sounds better with accidentals in or out.

Look at the example below:

- The key is D minor with its key signature of B♭. The 6th note is B♭, the 7th note is C.
- The 6th note could be raised to B♮, the 7th note could be raised to C♯.
- Play the example several times. Try leaving the accidentals out – you may prefer the sound.
- Remember: when you are composing, the choice is up to you.

Relative majors and minors

Major and minor keys with the same key signature as each other are called **relative majors** or **relative minors**. So E minor is the relative minor of G major, and G major is the relative major of E minor because they both have the same key signature of one sharp.

Relative majors and minors					
Major key	Key signature	Minor key	Major key	Key signature	Minor key
C	none	A	E	four sharps	C♯
G	one sharp	E	F	one flat	D
D	two sharps	B	B♭	two flats	G
A	three sharps	F♯	E♭	three flats	C
			A♭	four flats	F

What is the key of this piece?

Two ways of answering this question are:

1 By listening

There is really only one way to discover whether a piece is in a major or a minor key by listening, and that is *experience*. This means practice.

By listening to lots of major and minor chords (for chords, see Section 9, page 34) you soon learn to recognize a piece in which the key chord and other chords at important places are minor. The sound of the piece will be minor – and this brings you back to experience gained through practice. There is really no other way of learning to tell major from minor by ear. Remember that on page 27 you read: one feature that both the harmonic and the melodic minor scales have in common is that the 3rd note from the keynote is a semitone lower than the 3rd note in the major scale starting on the same note. This **minor 3rd** is the most important feature in hearing whether a piece of music is major or minor.

It is the 3rd note of a scale which makes a chord sound major or minor. So the more you practise listening to chords and scales, the better you will become at identifying major and minor.

2 By looking

To identify the key of a piece, first look at the key signature. The piece will be in one of two keys: either the major key with that key signature or the minor key with that key signature. Next, look at the notes which begin and end the piece. A piece is likely to end on its key note (this may be in the bass part, so look at all the notes in its last chord). A piece may or may not begin on its key note – it is worth looking at the beginning, but the ending is more reliable. Now look to see if there are any accidentals which might belong to the particular minor key you are checking. Are the 6th or 7th notes raised?

(NB Sometimes pieces change key (**modulate**) but this is outside the scope of this book.)

Put all this evidence together, and the name of the key should become obvious. For example:

- Look at the key signatures: both have 1 flat. Therefore the piece is in F major or in D minor.
- Look at the last note: example **A** ends on F; example **B** ends on D.
- Check for accidentals: example **A** has none; example **B** has B♮ and C♯.
- Result of investigation: example **A** is in F major; example **B** is in D minor.

The pentatonic scale

The **pentatonic scale** is one of the most universal scales. It is found in the music of Ireland and Scotland, eastern Europe, China, Japan and other places in the Far East, Africa, and in American plantation songs and spirituals.

The pentatonic scale has five notes to the octave and because it is an easy scale to work with, it is often used for children's songs and pieces.

The pentatonic scale pattern of tones and semitones is:

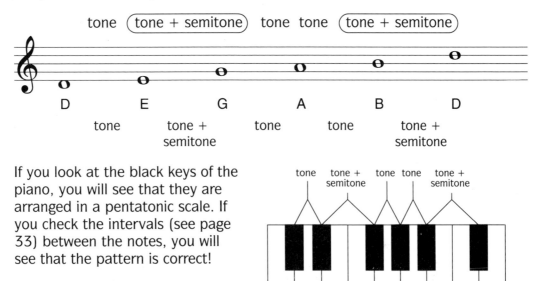

If you look at the black keys of the piano, you will see that they are arranged in a pentatonic scale. If you check the intervals (see page 33) between the notes, you will see that the pattern is correct!

Modes

Modes are a type of scale which were used in church and folk music from the earliest times. They are now used a great deal in rock and pop music, and also in jazz.

Two very popular and useful modes are the Aeolian mode and the Dorian mode.

The **Aeolian mode** has the same pattern of tones and semitones as a scale made by playing all the white notes on the piano from A to A.

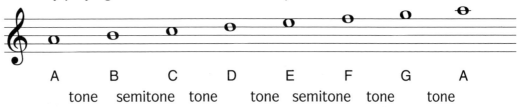

This does not mean that the Aeolian mode can only begin on A. The Aeolian mode can be built on any note by *copying this pattern of tones and semitones*.

A well-known melody in the Aeolian mode is *Greensleeves*.

The **Dorian mode** has the same pattern of tones and semitones as a scale made by playing all the white notes on the piano from D to D.

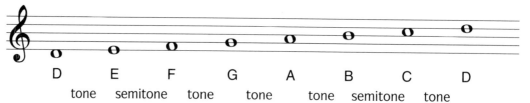

D	E	F	G	A	B	C	D
tone	semitone	tone	tone	tone	semitone	tone	

This does not mean that the Dorian mode can only begin on D. The Dorian mode can be built on any note by *copying this pattern of tones and semitones.*

A well-known tune in the Dorian mode is *Eleanor Rigby* by Lennon and McCartney.

You should play these modes until you are familiar with them before you try to use them in composing.

The names of the notes of the scale

Every note in a scale has a name by which it is known. Of course you can call the notes by their numbers (such as 5th, 2nd, and so on), but you may find the correct names useful when you are talking about music.

Below are two systems of naming the notes of a scale: **tonic solfa** and the **degrees of the scale.**

Note number	Tonic solfa	Degree
1st	doh	tonic
2nd	ray	supertonic
3rd	me	mediant
4th	fah	subdominant
5th	soh	dominant
6th	lah	submediant
7th	te	leading note
8th (1st)	doh	tonic

Intervals

An **interval** is the *distance in pitch* from one note to another. You already know two intervals by name:

> **semitone**: the smallest distance between any two notes on the keyboard
> **tone**: 2 next-door semitones

And you may also have met another interval with a special name:

> **octave**: the distance from any note to the next one with the same name

But we need to be able to describe the size of any interval so we can talk about them.

Intervals are measured and described by the number of letter-names between them including the first and the last. For example:

C-E is a **3rd**. Why? Because there are 3 letter-names between them – C, D, E

C-A is a **6th**. Why? Because there are 6 letter-names between them – C, D, E, F, G, A

Here are the intervals in the scale of C major:

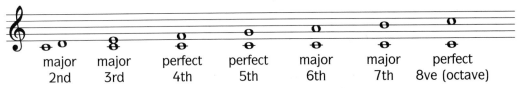

Intervals which are a semitone smaller than a major interval are described as 'minor'. Compare the intervals below with those in the scale of C major. Notice that each minor interval is one semitone smaller than its matching major interval above. Notice also that the 4th, the 5th and the 8ve do not change, but remain 'perfect'.

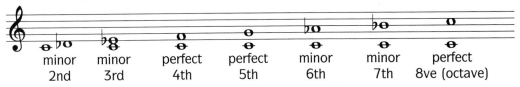

The intervals you are likely to need to know about are the ones which affect chords (see Section 9). These are the 3rds, 5ths, 6ths and possibly the 7ths. Look at the diagrams below and notice the difference between each pair of intervals (except the perfect 5th which is *never* major or minor, but always 'perfect').

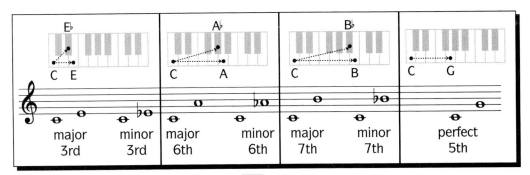

All about chords

What is a chord?

A **chord** is the name given to *two or more notes sounding together.*

The commonest type of chord is a 3-note chord called a **triad**. A triad has its notes arranged like this:

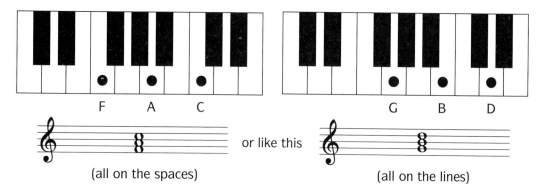

or like this

(all on the spaces)   (all on the lines)

As you can see, a triad is made up of a 3rd and a 5th above the bottom note (known as the **root**).

To play a triad you first find the bottom note (the root), then miss out the next note, play the next note, miss out the next note, and play the last note:

play one   miss one   play one   miss one   play one
(root)   (third)   (fifth)

When a triad is played with its notes sounding together like this, it is often known as a **block chord**.

Chord inversions (rearranging chords)

The three notes of a triad or chord can be arranged in any order – whatever sounds best is fine at this stage:

When a chord has its root on the bottom, it is said to be in **root position**.

When a chord has its third on the bottom, it is said to be in **first inversion**.

When a chord has its fifth on the bottom, it is said to be in **second inversion**.

Patterns with chords

Once you understand what a chord is, you can make backings and accompaniments for your melodies. Sometimes block chords are too heavy or solid for a piece, and something lighter is needed. Chords can be split up into their separate notes, and arranged into patterns called **riffs** or **broken chords**.

Look at the examples below. All these patterns are created from the chord of **C** which contains the notes **C**, **E** and **G**.

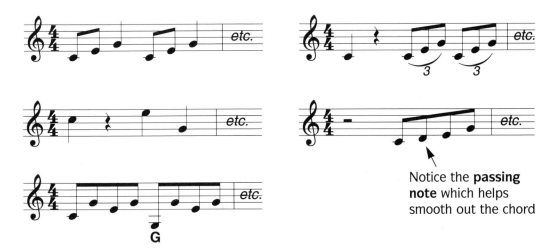

Notice the **passing note** which helps smooth out the chord

Naming chords

Chords can be built on any note of a major or minor scale. Here are the seven chords built on the notes of the C major scale:

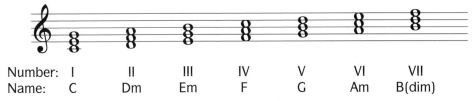

Number:	I	II	III	IV	V	VI	VII
Name:	C	Dm	Em	F	G	Am	B(dim)

Notice that each of these seven chords is named in two different ways:
a by a Roman numeral according to the number of the scale-note it is built on
b by its root-note name (the note of the scale upon which the chord is built) *and* its type, i.e. whether it is:

> major: a chord in which the interval between the root and the 3rd is 4 semitones (a major third)
>
> *or* minor: a chord in which the interval between the root and the 3rd is 3 semitones (a minor third). The chord will have a small 'm' after its root-note name to show it is minor.

dim (short for diminished) as in B(dim) is shown in brackets as it is a more advanced chord and outside the scope of this book.

Primary chords

In any major or minor scale, three chords or triads are used more often than the others. These are chords I, IV, and V. They are known as the **primary chords**.

Number:	I	II	III	IV	V	VI	VII
Name:	C	(Dm)	(Em)	F	G	(Am)	(Bdim)

Look again at the scale of C major shown above. The primary chords are C (I), F (IV) and G (V). These three chords between them contain every note of the major scale.

chord I (C) has C, E, G   chord IV (F) has F, A, C   chord V (G) has G, B, D

This means that every note of a melody composed in C major can be **harmonized** by at least one of the three primary chords (see below).

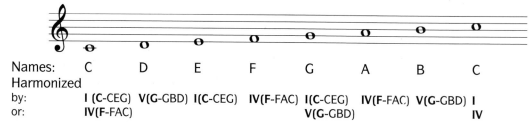

Names:	C	D	E	F	G	A	B	C
Harmonized by:	I (C-CEG)	V(G-GBD)	I(C-CEG)	IV(F-FAC)	I(C-CEG)	IV(F-FAC)	V(G-GBD)	I
or:	IV(F-FAC)				V(G-GBD)			IV

In just the same way, any piece in a major key can be harmonized by using only three chords – the three primary chords – provided it doesn't change key halfway through.

Secondary chords

The three primary chords are the most important chords in harmonizing a melody. But there are only three of them. To add colour and variety to the backing, the three **secondary chords** are used.

Look again at the chords of the scale of C:

Number:	I	II	III	IV	V	VI	VII
Name:	C	Dm	Em	F	G	Am	(Bdim)
Primary/ secondary:	P	S	S	P	P	S	•

The three secondary chords in a major key are chord II, chord III, and chord VI.

(NB Chord VII is a special case, and outside the scope of this book. Your teacher will explain it if you need to use it.)

Working out chords

To work out the primary and secondary chords of any key:

1   Play the scale or write out its notes.
2   Build triads on each note (except the 7th) by the 'play one, miss one, play one, miss one, play one' method, *or* write the three notes for each chord on the stave, remembering that in root position they *all* sit on lines, or *all* sit in spaces. (If you decide later you want to use the chord in an *inversion* – see page 34 – you will need to change the position of one or more of the three notes.)
3   Label the chords with their numbers or letter-names for easy reference.

Remember that major chords use only the letter-name of their root, but minor chords have a small 'm' after their letter-name. These labels are called the **chord symbols**.

Using chord symbols

One of the easiest ways of indicating backing chords to a melody is by writing the chord symbols over where they are needed on the stave.

Look at the example above and note:

- The key is G major. We know this from the key signature of F♯, and the ending on G (the key note).
- The primary chords are I (G), IV (C), V (D).
- The chord for the first bar is G. This is the key-chord and 'anchors' the piece in its own key.
- Bar 2 is harmonized by C, one of the primary chords.
- Bar 3 has two chords: Am, and D. D is another of the primary chords, but Am is not.
- Bar 4 has G. Note that a piece usually ends on its key-chord to make it sound satisfying.

Chords in common keys

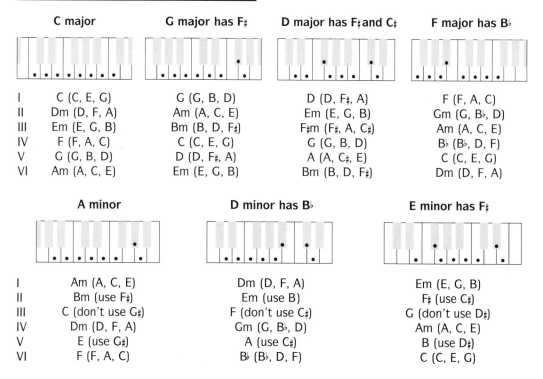

	C major	G major has F♯	D major has F♯ and C♯	F major has B♭
I	C (C, E, G)	G (G, B, D)	D (D, F♯, A)	F (F, A, C)
II	Dm (D, F, A)	Am (A, C, E)	Em (E, G, B)	Gm (G, B♭, D)
III	Em (E, G, B)	Bm (B, D, F♯)	F♯m (F♯, A, C♯)	Am (A, C, E)
IV	F (F, A, C)	C (C, E, G)	G (G, B, D)	B♭ (B♭, D, F)
V	G (G, B, D)	D (D, F♯, A)	A (A, C♯, E)	C (C, E, G)
VI	Am (A, C, E)	Em (E, G, B)	Bm (B, D, F♯)	Dm (D, F, A)

	A minor	D minor has B♭	E minor has F♯
I	Am (A, C, E)	Dm (D, F, A)	Em (E, G, B)
II	Bm (use F♯)	Em (use B)	F♯ (use C♯)
III	C (don't use G♯)	F (don't use C♯)	G (don't use D♯)
IV	Dm (D, F, A)	Gm (G, B♭, D)	Am (A, C, E)
V	E (use G♯)	A (use C♯)	B (use D♯)
VI	F (F, A, C)	B♭ (B♭, D, F)	C (C, E, G)

Note that:

● The extra sharp on the 7th note in minor scales is *always* used in chord V.
● Chords II and III in minor keys are tricky to use. It is probably better to keep to I, IV, V, and VI in minor keys at this stage.

Using chords in the Aeolian and Dorian modes

Both these modes are easy to harmonize. This is one reason why they are so much used in popular music.

Chords in the Aeolian mode:

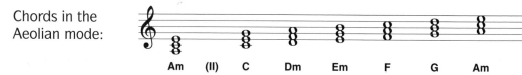

Am   (II)   C   Dm   Em   F   G   Am

(NB Chord II is not available in the Aeolian mode, but note that you can use chord VII.)

Chords in the Dorian mode:

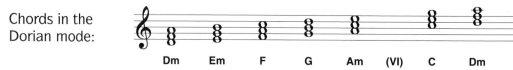

Dm   Em   F   G   Am   (VI)   C   Dm

(NB Chord VI is not available in the Dorian mode, but note that you use chord VII.)

Other modes are beyond the scope of this book.

Cadences

A piece of music usually (but not always) ends on its home chord (chord I). This makes the piece sound finished, and gives a satisfying ending.

The chord *before* the last chord is also important. It needs to lead on to the last chord in a way that 'announces' the ending.

These two final chords in any piece (or section of a piece) are known as a **cadence**.

Final cadences

There are two common cadences used to end a piece:

1   Chord V followed chord I is known as a **perfect cadence** (V-I).
2   Chord IV followed by chord I is known as a **plagal cadence** (IV-I).

The perfect cadence (V-I) is more common than the plagal cadence (IV-I), but there are no rules about which you should use. Let your ear be your guide when you are composing.

Look back at page 37. There you will see a melody written out with its backing chords. The key is G major. So chord V is based on D (D, F♯, A), and chord I is based on G (G, B, D). Chord IV is based on C (C, E, G). Notice that the last two chords are D and G. Therefore this piece ends with a perfect cadence.

Non-final cadences

Sometimes during a piece there is a feeling that the music has arrived somewhere, and yet the piece has not yet finished. It is as if the music is resting for a minute before continuing. This resting place is also a cadence, even though the music sounds 'unfinished'. In a cadence like this, the second chord will not be chord I.

There are two common 'unfinished' cadences used to end a *section* of a piece:

1   Chord I followed by chord V is known as an **imperfect cadence** (I-V).
     (The first chord can also be chord II, chord IV or even chord VI, but the second chord is always chord V.)
2   Chord V followed by chord VI is known as an **interrupted cadence** (V-VI).

Look at *Phil the Fluter's Ball* below. It is in the key of C. The chords in the key of C are set out below for reference:

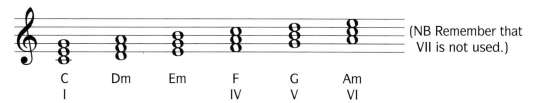

(NB Remember that VII is not used.)

C	Dm	Em	F	G	Am
I			IV	V	VI

Phil the Fluter's Ball

NB
- There are four phrases in the tune. Each phrase ends with a cadence or resting place.
- The last two chords of phrase 1 are F and C (IV and I). IV-I is a plagal cadence.
- The last two chords of phrase 2 are C and G (I and V). I-V is an imperfect cadence. (Remember that the important thing about an imperfect cadence is that the second chord is chord V.)
- The last two chords of phrase 3 are G and Am (V and VI). V-VI is an interrupted cadence.
- The last two chords of phrase 4 are G and C (V and I). V-I is a perfect cadence.

Play this piece through several times (with a partner, if necessary) and add the cadence chords. Repeat it until you can remember the sound of each cadence.

(NB The perfect cadence (V-I), and the imperfect cadence (I-V) are the two most important for you to learn now. Make sure you can recognize and use these first, and add the other two later on.)

Reference section

Common musical signs

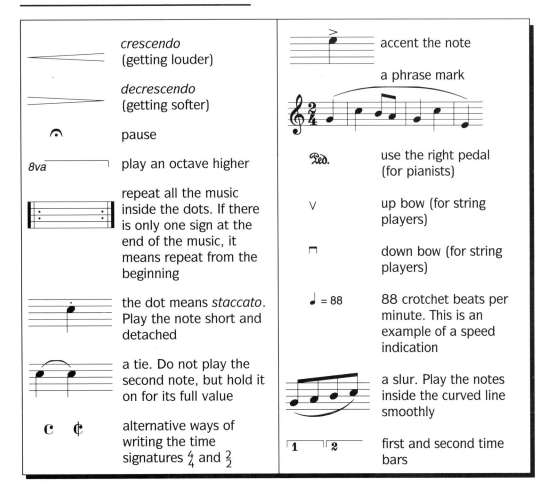

crescendo (getting louder)	accent the note
decrescendo (getting softer)	a phrase mark
pause	
8va play an octave higher	use the right pedal (for pianists)
repeat all the music inside the dots. If there is only one sign at the end of the music, it means repeat from the beginning	∨ up bow (for string players)
the dot means *staccato*. Play the note short and detached	down bow (for string players)
a tie. Do not play the second note, but hold it on for its full value	♩ = 88 88 crotchet beats per minute. This is an example of a speed indication
c **¢** alternative ways of writing the time signatures 4/4 and 2/2	a slur. Play the notes inside the curved line smoothly
	1 2 first and second time bars

Different types of ornament

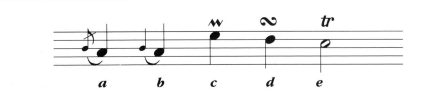

a   b   c   d   e

a   *acciaccatura:* play the 'crushed' note as quickly as possible

b   *appoggiatura:* give the small note half the value of the main note

c   *mordent:* play the main note, the note above, and the main note as quickly as possible. (Think of a mordent as a little 'twiddle'.)

d   *turn:* a 'turn around the note'. Play the note above, the main note, the note below, the main note as a decoration.

e   *trill:* as fast as possible, play the main note and the note above one after the other as many times as you can fit into the value of the main note.

Common musical words explained

Words affecting tempo

accel., accelerando	getting faster	*moderato*	at a moderate speed
adagio	slow and unhurried		
allegretto	rather fast	*più mosso*	more movement, faster
allegro	quick and lively		
andante	at a walking pace	*presto*	fast
animato	animated, lively	*prestissimo*	very fast
con moto	with movement	*rall., rallentando*	getting slower
grave	slow and solemn	*ritard., ritardando*	getting slower
largo	very broad, slow and dignified	*rit., ritenuto*	getting slower
		tempo	the speed of the music
lento	slow		
meno mosso	less movement, slower	*a tempo*	in time
		vivace	lively

Words affecting dynamics

cres., crescendo	getting louder	*forzando, fz, sforzando, sfz*	strongly accented
decres., decrescendo	gradually getting softer	*marcato*	marked
dim., diminuendo	gradually getting softer	*mezzo forte, mf*	moderately loud
		mezzo piano, mp	moderately soft
forte, f	loud	*morendo*	dying away
fortiss., fortissimo, ff	very loud	*piano, p*	soft
		pianissimo, pp	very soft

Words affecting expression and mood

animato	animatedly	*maestoso*	grand and majestic
brio	energy and vigour		
cantabile	in a singing style	*mesto*	sadly
dolce	sweetly	*pesante*	heavy
espressivo, espress.	expressively	*scherzando*	playfully
grazioso	gracefully	*staccato*	short and detached
legato, leg.	smoothly		
leggiero, legg.	lightly	*tranquillo*	calmly

Words affecting instrumental technique

arco	with the bow (string players)	*pizz., pizzicato*	plucked with the finger (strings)
con ped.	with the right pedal (piano)	*senza vibrato*	without vibrato (strings)
con sordini	with mutes (strings or brass)	*tre corde*	without the left pedal (piano)
glissando, gliss.	sliding up or down the notes	*una corda*	with the left pedal (piano)
L.H. and R. H.	left hand and right hand (piano)		

Words indicating the way around the music

coda ⊕	an ending section	*dal segno, D.S*	repeat from the sign
da capo, D.C.,	repeat from the		(%) to 'Fine' (the end)
D.C. al Fine	beginning as far as the	*fine*	the end
	word 'Fine' (the end)	*tutti*	all, everyone plays
		V.S.	turn over the page quickly

Useful supporting words and phrases

con	with	*poco a poco*	little by little, gradually
ma non troppo	but not too much		
meno	less	*sempre*	always
molto	much, very	*senza*	without
più	more	*subito*	suddenly
poco	a little		

Words describing instruments, singers and their groups

alto, contralto — A female voice with a low range of notes. 'Alto' also applies to instruments with the same range.

baritone — A male voice with a range of notes a little higher than a bass voice; instruments with the same range.

bass — The lowest male voice; the lowest instrument in its family.

bass guitar — A 4-stringed electric guitar used for playing the bass line in rock/pop music.

bassoon — A woodwind instrument with a double reed. It has the same range as the cello.

brass — A family of blown metal instruments found in bands and orchestras, including the trumpet, cornet, trombone, etc.

cello — The tenor instrument of the string family. It is held between the knees and played with a bow.

choir — An organized group of singers who rehearse and perform together.

chorus — There are several meanings for 'chorus'. Two are: (i) a choir of singers; (ii) part of a song repeated after every verse.

clarinet — The alto member of the woodwind family, with a single reed, popular in both jazz and classical music.

cornet — A brass instrument with a bright tone which resembles a small trumpet in appearance.

counter-tenor — A very high and rare male voice.

double bass — The bass instrument of the string family. It is sometimes called a string bass in popular music.

drums — The set of drums used in a rock band.

duet — A piece for two performers.

flute — The soprano member of the woodwind family. It is held horizontally and blown across the mouth-piece.

French horn — A member of the brass family with three valves, and a long tube wound round in a coil.

gamelan — Indonesian gong orchestra.

glockenspiel	A percussion instrument played by striking metal bars with beaters.
harpsichord	An early keyboard instrument overtaken in the 18th century by the piano. The plucked strings produce a 'twangy' sound.
keyboards	One or more synthesizers or electronic keyboards used in a rock or pop group, usually racked and played by a single performer.
lead guitar	An electric guitar used for playing lead melodies in rock/pop music.
lute	An early plucked string instrument with a pear-shaped body, and a fretted finger-board.
marimba	A Latin-American instrument similar to a xylophone, but with metal bars and a mellower tone.
oboe	A woodwind instrument with a double reed, and a nasal, reedy tone.
percussion	A family of instruments which are played by hitting or striking.
recorder	An ancient woodwind instrument still popular today. Five types of recorder are in common use: sopranino, descant, treble, tenor, bass.
quartet	A piece for four performers.
quintet	A piece for five performers.
rhythm guitar	An electric guitar used for playing chords in rock/pop music.
saxophone	A keyed wind instrument mainly used in popular music.
solo	A piece, or section of a piece, for a single performer.
soprano	The highest female voice.
string quartet	A group consisting of two violins, viola and cello.
strings	An orchestral family consisting of violins, violas, cellos, double basses.
synthesizer	A complex electronic sound generator which is usually operated from a keyboard. Used mainly in rock/pop music.
tenor	A high male voice.
timpani	Large, bowl-shaped tunable drums. Sometimes called kettle drums.
treble	An unbroken boy's voice.
trio	(i) Piece for three performers (ii) Middle section of a minuet and trio.
trombone	A brass instrument operated by a slide with a similar pitch to a cello.
trumpet	A brass instrument with a bright tone found in orchestras and bands.
tuba	A very large brass instrument playing the lowest notes in the orchestra or band.
vibes, vibraphone	A large instrument like a glockenspiel, but the tone is electrically enhanced.
viola	The alto member of the string family. Slightly larger than a violin.
violin	The smallest and highest member of the string family.
viol	A family of stringed instruments popular in the 15th-17th centuries, overtaken by the development of the violin.
woodwind	An orchestral family whose main members are flute, oboe, clarinet, bassoon.
xylophone	An instrument with wooden bars played by striking them with beaters.

Words for musical styles and genres (types)

a cappella	Unaccompanied singing.
aria	A vocal solo found in opera and oratorios.
arrangement	The rearranging of a piece of music to make it possible to play with different instruments from those it was written for. Extra parts are often added.

baroque music	Music from the 17th and 18th centuries. Some famous baroque composers are J S Bach, Handel, Vivaldi, Scarlatti.
blues	A solo song based on a 12-bar chord sequence, and using the 'blues scale' which contains a minor 3rd and a minor 7th. See also *twelve-bar blues*.
cadenza	A showy improvised or written out passage for a soloist.
canon	A piece in which each part has the same or similar music, but enters one after the other. A canon is like a round, but has a coda at the end so that all parts stop together.
cantata	A longer work for singers and orchestra consisting of several pieces on the same theme (e.g. 'Spring'), each performed by soloists or choir, and accompanied by instruments.
chamber music	Music for a small group of players suitable for performing in a room.
classical music	(i) Music from the 17th and 18th centuries. Some famous classical composers are Mozart and Beethoven; (ii) A term applied to 'serious' music as opposed to 'popular' music.
concerto	A longer work for orchestra and a soloist.
concerto grosso	A baroque work where a small group of soloists is contrasted with a larger orchestral group. This type of music was popular in the 17th and 18th centuries.
country and western	American folk music such as cowboy songs played on guitars, ukuleles, banjos etc.
lied, lieder	German 19th-century song where the piano accompaniment is as important as the vocal line.
madrigal	A secular (non-religious) song in several parts popular in England in Elizabethan times.
march	A piece for marching in duple or quadruple time in a rousing mood.
mass	A Catholic church service in several sections often set to music for choir and/or soloists e.g. Mozart's 'Coronation Mass'.
minuet and trio	The minuet was a popular 18th-century court dance in triple time. It was usually repeated after a central 'trio'.
motet	A religious piece for a choir.
opera	A play set to music for soloists, chorus and orchestra.
oratorio	A large work for choir, soloists and orchestra based on a religious theme e.g. Handel's 'Messiah'.
overture	A piece to introduce an opera, oratorio, musical show, or concert.
pavane	A slow stately dance in duple time, popular from the 16th-18th centuries.
plainsong	An early type of church music sung in unison unacccompanied, in a free time to match the rhythm of the words.
prelude	An introduction. Sometimes a whole piece is called a prelude, e.g. Chopin's Preludes.
programme music	Music which tells a story, or paints a picture or a mood in sound.
recitative, recit.	Used in opera or oratorio between the main numbers to tell the story. Sung in speech rhythm by a soloist.
rhythm 'n' blues	A type of music which combines jazz and blues.
Romantic music	Music from the 19th century which is more concerned with expressing a mood than with structure or form.

rondo	A form in music where the main theme keeps returning, rather like the chorus in a song.
round	A piece in which each part has the same or similar music, but performers enter one after the other. Unlike the canon, a round has no coda at the end so that the ending has to be planned.
serial music	See *twelve-tone music*.
sonata	A work for a solo instrument, often with a piano accompaniment, in several sections.
song cycle	A series of songs on a particular theme or story. Schubert wrote some famous examples.
suite	A set of pieces written to be played together. In the 17th and 18th centuries a suite was a set of dances in the same or related keys.
symphony	A large-scale work in several movements (sections) for full orchestra. Beethoven wrote nine.
theme and variations	A set of pieces all based on the same main theme which is played first.
twelve-bar blues	An instrumental piece based on a 12-bar chord sequence, using the 'blues scale' which contains a minor 3rd and a minor 7th. See also *blues*.
twelve-tone music	A composition based on a pre-arrangement of the twelve semitones in an octave in several different orders known as 'series'. The music is not in any key, and is said to be 'atonal'.
waltz	A dance in triple time with an oom-pah-pah rhythm.

Words affecting form and structure

anacrusis	An upbeat. Often used to describe an incomplete bar at the beginning of a piece.
backing	Another word for accompaniment used in pop and rock music.
binary form	A two-section piece where the first section is answered by the second section.
busk	(i) to entertain in the streets; (ii) to make music up as you go along i.e. to improvise.
chord progression, sequence	A series of chords with a particular importance.
chord symbols	A way of indicating chords used in popular music. Each chord consists of one or more letters, and may have a figure e.g. Fm⁷.
chromatic scale	A scale in which every interval is a semitone.
counter-melody	A second melody played together with the main melody.
descant	A counter-melody added above the main melody.
drone	A bass part on one or two notes which imitates the drone notes on bagpipes.
episode	A section between repeats of the main theme.
figured bass	A bass line with the required chords shown underneath in figures.
ground bass	A bass line which is constantly repeated throughout the piece e.g. Pachelbel's 'Canon'.
harmonize	To add the chords to a melody.
imitation	A musical device where one part imitates another. The imitation may not necessarily be exact.

improvise	To play without music, and make it up as you go along. An improvisation may be based on an existing theme.
lyrics	A term used in popular music for the words of a song.
modes	A system of scales used before the 17th century when it was replaced by the major and minor scales. Each mode has a different pattern of tones and semitones.
modulation	A change of key.
movement	A complete section of a large-scale piece.
octave	The distance in pitch from one note to the next one with the same name.
opus	A numbering system for the works of a composer e.g. Op 42.
ostinato	A short repeated pattern of notes.
pedal note	A bass note which holds on as the harmony changes above it.
repetition	An exact repeat.
ternary form	A three-part form where the first part is repeated to make the third (ABA).
unison	Two or more instruments or voices playing the same part.
vamp	To improvise an accompaniment, usually to a song.
whole-tone scale	A scale with six notes where each interval is a tone.

Words and rhythms

Sometimes a song just seems to grow by itself and pops into your mind with the words and music complete. But if all you have are the words it is important to sort the basics out first.

- The first basic is to match up the important words or syllables (sections of words) with the strong beats in the music. If you chant the words aloud, and tap a beat on your knee at the same time, you will find that the beat falls naturally on the important words or syllables. For example:

  A <u>pie</u> and <u>chips</u> will <u>make</u> me <u>fat</u> and <u>ice</u> - cream <u>makes</u> me <u>fat</u> - ter, ___
  But <u>noth</u> - ing <u>piles</u> the <u>weight</u> on <u>like</u> a <u>piece</u> of <u>cod</u> in <u>bat</u> - ter. ___

- Notice also that once you start chanting the words, you need an extra beat after each line to keep the rhythm steady and balanced. This is not necessary for every set of words, but tapping the beat as you chant will soon tell you whether you need it or not.

- Once you have your strong syllables underlined, you must choose a time signature and place the barlines *in front of* the strong syllables. You could choose almost any time signature, depending on the mood you want:

$\frac{2}{4}$ A |<u>pie</u> and |<u>chips</u> will |<u>make</u> me |<u>fat</u> and |<u>ice</u> - cream |<u>makes</u> me |<u>fat</u> - ter,|___

$\frac{3}{4}$ A |<u>pie</u> and |<u>chips</u> will |<u>make</u> me |<u>fat</u> and |<u>ice</u> - cream |<u>makes</u> me |<u>fat</u> - ter,|___

$\frac{6}{8}$ A |<u>pie</u> and <u>chips</u> will |<u>make</u> me <u>fat</u> and |<u>ice</u> - cream <u>makes</u> me |<u>fat</u> - ter, ___

$\frac{4}{4}$ A |<u>pie</u> and <u>chips</u> will |<u>make</u> me <u>fat</u> and |<u>ice</u> - cream <u>makes</u> me |<u>fat</u> - ter, __

● Notice that you do not need a complete bar at the start. However, if the piece begins with an incomplete bar, the last bar loses the value of the first bar so the two of them together add up to one complete bar – see anacrusis on page 17.

● Also notice that the barlines are in exactly the same place for $\frac{2}{4}$ and $\frac{3}{4}$, and for $\frac{6}{8}$ and $\frac{4}{4}$. The difference comes when you choose note values for each syllable. You may like to try them all out and decide which rhythm is the most suitable for the mood of your song, e.g.:

$\frac{2}{4}$ A |pie and |chips will |make me |fat and |ice - cream |makes me |fat - ter, |___

$\frac{3}{4}$ A |pie and |chips will |make me |fat and |ice - cream |makes me |fat - ter, |___

$\frac{6}{8}$ A |pie and chips will |make me fat and |ice - cream makes me |fat - ter, ___

$\frac{4}{4}$ A |pie and chips will |make me fat and |ice - cream makes me |fat - ter, ___

● Once you have your rhythm worked out, and you have checked that each bar adds up to the time signature correctly, you can go ahead and write your melody. This will be more musical and interesting if you make some of the crotchets into pairs of quavers or other notes, and vary your rhythm as much as possible, but you will discover this as you go.

There are other ways of fitting words to music, but this is a basic way to start until you become more experienced.

Keyboard chart

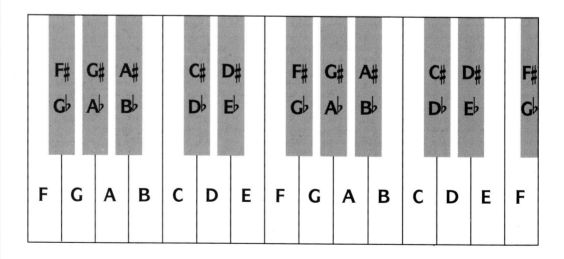